CON EC

EXPLORING SPACE
AND BEYOND

DEMOTING PLUTO

THE DISCOVERY OF THE DWARF PLANETS

by Steve Kortenkamp

CAPSTONE PRESS
a capstone imprint

Connect Books are published by Capstone Press,
1710 Roe Crest Drive,
North Mankato, Minnesota 56003
www.capstonepub.com

Library of Congress Cataloging-in-Publication Data
Kortenkamp, Steve, author.
  Demoting Pluto : the discovery of the dwarf planets / Steve Kortenkamp.
      pages cm. — (Exploring space and beyond)
  Summary: "Describes the dwarf planet Pluto and the 2006 decision to change its
status from a regular planet"—Provided by publisher.
  Audience: Ages 8–14.
  Audience: Grades 4 to 6.
  Includes bibliographical references and index.
  ISBN 978-1-4914-4162-6 (library binding)
  ISBN 978-1-4914-4176-3 (paperback)
  ISBN 978-1-4914-4182-4 (eBook pdf)
  1. Dwarf planets—Juvenile literature. 2. Pluto (Dwarf planet)—Juvenile
literature. I. Title.
  QB701.K55 2016
  523.49'22—dc23
                              2015017741

Editorial Credits
Abby Colich, editor; Kyle Grenz, designer; Wanda Winch, media researcher;
Tori Abraham, production specialist

Photo Credits
Black Cat Studios: Ron Miller, 13, 18, 36-37; Capstone, 5 (bottom); Corbis:
Bettmann, 17; Getty Images: UIG/BSIP, 10; International Astronomical Union:
Robert Hurt (SSC), 22-23; NASA, 33, NASA: ESA, A. Feild (STScl), 42-43,
ESA, G. Bacon (STScl), 19, ESA, A. Schaller (STScl), 34-35, ESA/E. Olszewski,
University of Arizona, 44-45 (background), JHUAPL/SwRI, 26-27, JPL, 14, JPL-
Caltech, 7, 20, 31, JPL-Caltech/Robert Hurt (IPAC), 21, JPL-Caltech/UCLA/
MPS/DLR/IDA, 29; Science Source: Chris Butler, 9, Detlev van Ravenswaay, 5
(top), John R. Foster, 39, Take 27 Ltd, 8, The International Astronomical Union/
Martin Kornmesser, 41; Shutterstock: Elenarts, cover (top), Ian Doktor, space
background, MichaelTaylor, cover (bottom), Tristan3D, 12, Vadim Sadovski, 25

Printed in the United States of America in Stevens Point, Wisconsin
032015   008824WZF15

Table of Contents

What's in Space?

Do you ever look at the sky and wonder what's out there? You may know about the planets, the sun, and the moon. But there are actually billions of other objects in our **solar system**. Some are giant. Others are tiny. They **orbit** the sun along with the eight planets and their moons. How do scientists know what all these objects are? Sometimes they're not sure at first.

One of the objects orbiting the sun is the dwarf planet Pluto. For 76 years scientists considered Pluto to be the ninth planet in our solar system. Then they found another object similar to Pluto. Was the other object, called Eris, also a planet? Scientists weren't sure. If Eris wasn't a planet, then was Pluto also not a planet? To answer that question, scientists had to come up with rules to decide what makes an object a planet or a dwarf planet.

Today, Eris and Pluto, along with three other objects in space—Ceres, Haumea, and Makemake—are known as the dwarf planets. A dwarf planet is round and orbits the sun like a planet. But they are found in areas with many other objects that aren't planets, such as asteroids.

What we know about objects in space is always changing. Scientists learn new things every day. They make many observations before deciding if a space object is a dwarf planet.

solar system—the sun and the objects that move around it; our solar system has eight planets, five dwarf planets including Pluto, and many moons, asteroids, and comets

orbit—the path an object follows as it goes around the sun or a planet

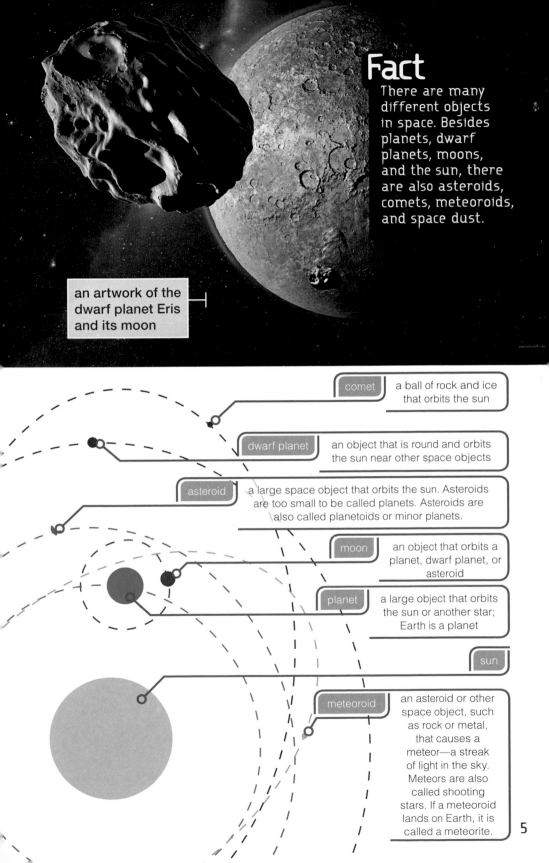

Fact

There are many different objects in space. Besides planets, dwarf planets, moons, and the sun, there are also asteroids, comets, meteoroids, and space dust.

an artwork of the dwarf planet Eris and its moon

comet — a ball of rock and ice that orbits the sun

dwarf planet — an object that is round and orbits the sun near other space objects

asteroid — a large space object that orbits the sun. Asteroids are too small to be called planets. Asteroids are also called planetoids or minor planets.

moon — an object that orbits a planet, dwarf planet, or asteroid

planet — a large object that orbits the sun or another star; Earth is a planet

sun

meteoroid — an asteroid or other space object, such as rock or metal, that causes a meteor—a streak of light in the sky. Meteors are also called shooting stars. If a meteoroid lands on Earth, it is called a meteorite.

The Making of the Solar System

To understand dwarf planets and other space objects, we must first know how they were formed. To do this, we need to look far back in time.

Five billion years ago, our solar system didn't yet exist. In its place was a huge cloud of gas. This gas cloud was more than 6 trillion miles (10 trillion kilometers) across. Mixed in with the gas cloud was tons of dust. Slowly the cloud began to collapse, like a balloon shrinking as air leaks out. Most of the gas and dust in the shrinking cloud piled together. It got very hot. When the temperature in the center reached millions of degrees, the gas started to burn. Our sun was born.

Fact
Six trillion miles is a lot! That's a six followed by 12 zeros—6,000,000,000,000.

an artwork of what the solar system may have looked like when forming

7

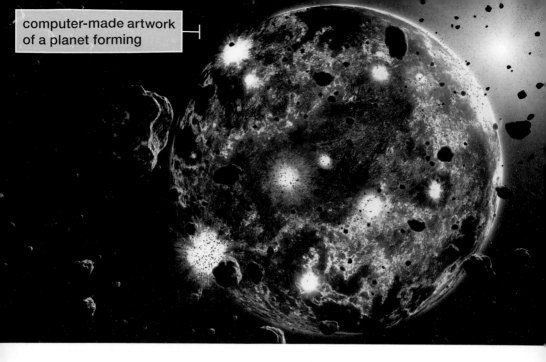

computer-made artwork of a planet forming

Gravity caused some of the gas and dust left in the shrinking cloud to orbit close to the new sun. The dust began sticking together and forming small rocks. The rocks clumped together into boulders that got bigger and bigger. Soon hundreds of round objects grew from the boulders. After about 100 million years, most of the round objects had crashed together. They formed Mercury, Venus, Earth, and Mars. Today scientists call these first four planets, which are closest to the sun, the **inner planets**.

After the inner planets formed, a lot of rocks and boulders were left over. Today these rocks and boulders are known as asteroids. About a million asteroids are orbiting the sun in the **asteroid belt**. Only one of the leftover objects in the asteroid belt is round. It orbits the sun near the asteroids. This is the dwarf planet Ceres.

inner planets—the four planets closest to the sun—Mercury, Venus, Earth, and Mars

asteroid belt—the area in space between Mars and Jupiter where the most asteroids are found

The gas and dust that were farthest from the sun were much colder. This outer part was so cold that some of the gas froze into ice. It then mixed with the dust and rocks. Bigger planets grew from this material. The bigger planets had stronger gravity that pulled in a lot of gas from the cloud. Jupiter, Saturn, Uranus, and Neptune formed this way. Scientists call these the **outer planets**.

outer planets—the four planets farthest from the sun—Jupiter, Saturn, Uranus, and Neptune

an artwork showing the formation of the solar system

After the outer planets formed, a lot of dust, ice, and rocks were left over. Today most of the objects that formed from this material orbit the sun beyond Neptune. These objects form the **trans-neptunian region**. Four out of the five known dwarf planets are found in this area.

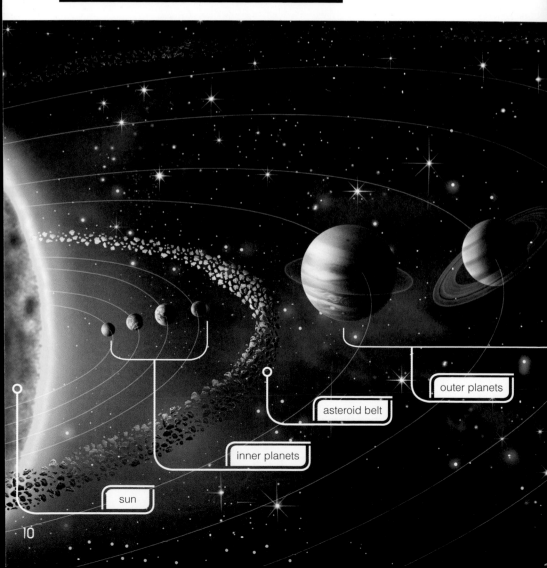

outer planets

asteroid belt

inner planets

sun

These frozen chunks of ice, dust, and rock are more than 30 times farther from the sun than Earth. That's about 3 billion miles (5 billion km) away. Neptune sometimes pulls these objects closer to the sun. As they warm up, they give off gas and dust and turn into comets.

Pluto, Makemake, and Haumea, along with most of the other trans-neptunian objects, are in a region of space called the **Kuiper belt**. The Kuiper belt stretches from Neptune out to about 50 times farther from the sun than Earth.

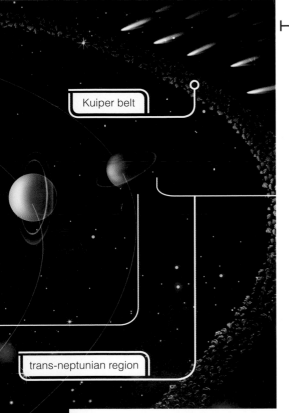

Kuiper belt

trans-neptunian region

The solar system is so large that scientists have divided it into sections.

Fact
The dwarf planet Eris only passes through the Kuiper belt during part of its orbit around the sun. The rest of the time it orbits outside of the Kuiper belt.

trans-neptunian region—an area of space objects that orbit the sun beyond the planet Neptune

Kuiper belt—the area of the solar system between about 30 and 50 times farther from the sun than Earth. Pluto and thousands of other icy objects are in the Kuiper belt.

Discovering Space Objects

For thousands of years, people have known about the five planets closest to the sun besides Earth. Mercury, Venus, Mars, Jupiter, and Saturn can all be seen at night without a telescope.

Then in 1781 astronomers discovered Uranus. William and Caroline Herschel, a brother and sister who worked together, were the first people to spot it. Through their small telescope, Uranus looked pale blue. It moved slowly past stars in the sky.

an artwork of the planet Uranus

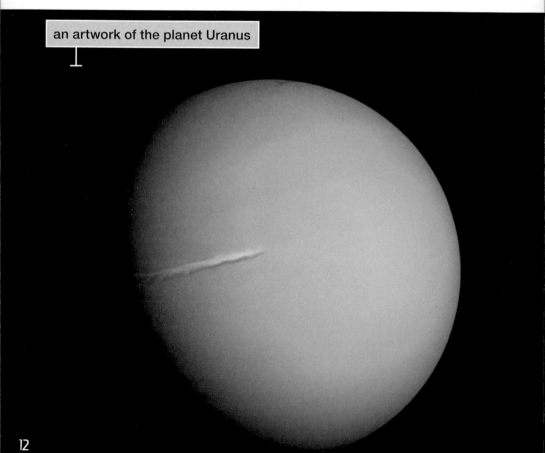

an illustration of Ceres

After the discovery of Uranus, scientists began studying the distances between all known planets. There seemed to be a large, empty gap between Mars and Jupiter. Many astronomers thought another planet might be orbiting the sun between them.

All over the world, astronomers began searching the sky with their telescopes, looking for the new planet. On New Year's Day in 1801, Italian astronomer Giuseppe Piazzi finally found the new planet. He named it Ceres after the Roman goddess of harvests. For many years, Ceres was considered a planet in our solar system.

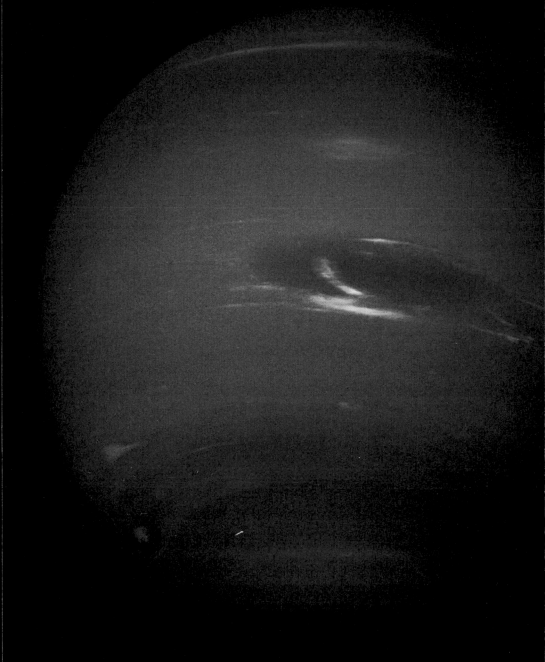

photo of Neptune taken
by the NASA space
probe *Voyager 2*

Astronomers could see Ceres slowly moving past the stars. Then they started finding more planets nearby. In just six years, they found three more planets between Mars and Jupiter. All of these new planets were very tiny compared to Earth. In fact, they were even smaller than Earth's moon. They were the smallest planets in our solar system. By 1845 there were 12 known planets.

Then scientists began searching for a 13th planet beyond Uranus. More than 60 years after its discovery, scientists were very puzzled by Uranus. The planet slowly orbited the sun, but it moved differently than the other planets. At first Uranus seemed to orbit too fast. Later it seemed to orbit too slowly.

Two mathematicians in Europe believed that gravity from an unseen planet must be pulling on Uranus. They said this was causing it to move in an odd way. But astronomers didn't believe them right away. They didn't look for the planet.

Finally in 1846 German astronomers heard this idea about another planet. Once they knew where to look, it only took 30 minutes to discover the 13th planet. They named it Neptune.

Just three years later, in 1849, the number of known planets shot up to 18. Astronomers had discovered five more planets between Mars and Jupiter. That's when they first started to believe that too many objects were being called planets. Most astronomers thought that all of the tiny objects between Mars and Jupiter, including Ceres, should be called asteroids. This is in the area now known as the asteroid belt. Asteroids orbit the sun like planets do, but are not always round. Ceres had been called a planet for almost 50 years. Now it would be called an asteroid.

By 1851 the number of objects considered planets was down to eight. These were Mercury, Venus, Earth, Mars, Jupiter, Saturn, Uranus, and Neptune. These are the same eight planets we have today.

Even with so many planets now considered asteroids, scientists still believed there were more planets out there. Both Uranus and Neptune seemed to move oddly compared with the other planets. Astronomers thought gravity from another object orbiting the sun beyond Neptune caused this. They called the mysterious object "Planet X." Astronomers all over the world spent many years searching for Planet X.

On February 18, 1930, Clyde Tombaugh, an American astronomer working in Arizona, discovered Planet X. Astronomers named the new planet Pluto.

Fact

The 18 planets in the year 1849 were Mercury, Venus, Earth, Mars, Ceres, Pallas, Juno, Vesta, Astraea, Hebe, Iris, Flora, Metis, Hygiea, Jupiter, Saturn, Uranus, and Neptune.

Clyde Tombaugh, discoverer of Pluto, with his telescope in 1930

PLUTO FEVER

Astronomers held a contest to find a name for Planet X. Eleven-year-old schoolgirl Venetia Burney won the contest. She chose the name Pluto. Excitement over the discovery of Pluto quickly spread. Nuclear scientists named a new element "plutonium" after the planet. Disney's big-eared rodent Mickey Mouse soon made friends with a lovable hound named Pluto.

CHAPTER 3

Defining Planets

For the next 70 years, Pluto was considered the ninth planet in our solar system. Using bigger and better telescopes, astronomers studied Pluto. They learned that it is very tiny compared with the other planets.

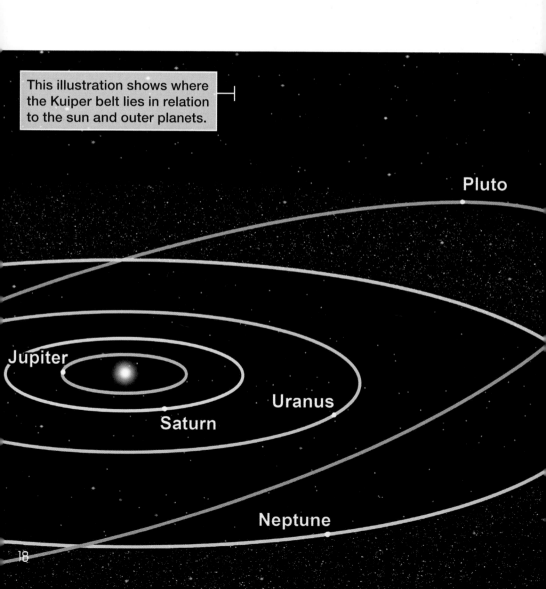

This illustration shows where the Kuiper belt lies in relation to the sun and outer planets.

Pluto

Jupiter

Uranus

Saturn

Neptune

artwork of an object in the Kuiper belt

Kuiper Belt

In the 1990s astronomers began discovering thousands of icy asteroids beyond Neptune. In 1992 astronomers David Jewitt and Jane Luu were working with a mountaintop telescope on the island of Hawaii. On August 30, 1992, they announced they had found a small icy object in the trans-neptunian region. Just a few months later they discovered another. At that point astronomers knew that Pluto was not alone. Jewitt and Luu had discovered the Kuiper belt.

Uranus, Neptune and Pluto

In 1986 Voyager 2 revealed the true nature of Uranus (top left), which lays on its side between the orbits of Saturn and Neptune. Uranus has a bevy of narrow rings and astounding moons. Since 1993 JPL's Wide-Field and Planetary Camera (WFPC2) on NASA's Hubble Space Telescope has continued to observe Uranus.

In 1989 Voyager 2 sped past Neptune (top right), discovering narrow rings and many small satellites. Neptune is the windiest planet, with winds blowing at speeds over 2,400 kilometers (1,500 miles) per hour.

Distant Pluto and its moon Charon—30 to 50 times farther from the Sun than Earth is— have not been visited by spacecraft. The European Space Agency's Faint Camera on NASA's Hubble Space Telescope provided this view (bottom).

Mike Brown and his team have made many discoveries.

Before announcing their discovery in 1992, Jane Luu told a young student named Mike Brown about the discovery. Brown became fascinated with finding more objects in the Kuiper belt. Eventually he formed his own team of astronomers. They went on to discover Haumea in 2004 as well as Eris and Makemake in 2005.

When Mike Brown and his team discovered Eris in 2005, it became a huge problem. Eris is about the same size as Pluto. Astronomers didn't know if Eris should be called a planet also.

an artwork of the dwarf planet Eris and its moon, Dysnomia

By this time astronomers had discovered hundreds of icy objects in the Kuiper belt. Pluto was now just one object among the hundreds. Astronomers started to question whether Pluto should still be called a planet.

In 2006 astronomers gathered to vote on how to decide if an object was a planet or not. They created three rules to help them make this decision. A planet had to follow all three rules or else it would be considered a dwarf planet, an asteroid, or a moon.

1. A planet must orbit the sun. It can't orbit another planet or any other object. Earth's moon cannot be a planet because it orbits Earth, not the sun.

2. A planet must be round. It can't have an uneven or crooked shape. Most asteroids are not round, so they cannot be planets.

3. A planet cannot have any other objects, such as asteroids, orbiting the sun with it.

Members of the International Astronomical Union (IAU) vote on what it means to call something a planet in 2006.

The third rule is the most important. Because of Eris, and the thousands of other icy trans-neptunian objects nearby, Pluto could no longer be considered a planet. Instead, scientists now consider both Pluto and Eris to be dwarf planets. On August 24, 2006, Pluto officially became known as a dwarf planet. Two other objects Mike Brown discovered, Makemake and Haumea, would also be called dwarf planets.

The rules also apply to Ceres in the asteroid belt. Ceres is round. It is not jagged like the asteroids near it. After first being called a planet, then an asteroid, Ceres would now be called a dwarf planet. Because Ceres is round, it is a dwarf planet.

Fact

The astronomers who decided whether an object was a planet or not were members of the International Astronomical Union (IAU). More than 11,000 astronomers belong to the IAU.

CHAPTER 4

Studying Pluto

What scientists know about Pluto has changed over the years. The more science advances, the more there is to learn about the former ninth planet.

When Clyde Tombaugh discovered Pluto in 1930, everyone thought it was about the same size as Earth. They couldn't tell for sure because Pluto was so far away. As telescopes got stronger, astronomers could more carefully study Pluto. They started to learn that it was actually much smaller than Earth.

By 1950 they thought Pluto might be about the same size as Mars, which is about half the size of Earth. By 1976 they thought it might be about the same size as Earth's moon, which is about one-fourth the size of Earth. The more scientists learned about Pluto, the smaller and smaller they realized it was.

In 1978 astronomers discovered a moon orbiting Pluto. By studying how the moon, named Charon, moves, scientists can tell how strong Pluto's gravity is. The strength of its gravity tells them about how big Pluto really is. They learned that Pluto is about 1,400 miles (2,300 km) across. This is only about two-thirds the size of Earth's moon. That's about half the distance from New York to California.

Charon is not orbiting Pluto alone. Astronomers recently discovered four other tiny moons orbiting Pluto. They are named Nix, Hydra, Kerberos, and Styx.

an artwork of the
dwarf planet Pluto

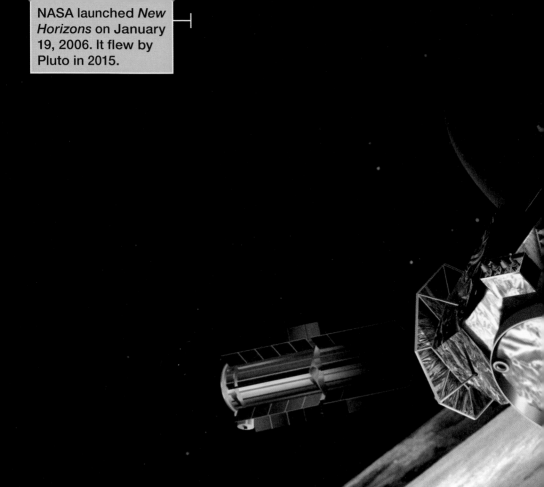

NASA launched *New Horizons* on January 19, 2006. It flew by Pluto in 2015.

Pluto is very far away from the sun. From Pluto's surface, the sun looks like a bright star in a dark sky. Astronomers have a difficult time taking pictures of Pluto. The best pictures are from the **Hubble Space Telescope**. These pictures show that Pluto has mysterious light and dark patches on its surface.

In July 2015 the **space probe** *New Horizons* flew past Pluto and its moon Charon. Cameras on *New Horizons* took pictures and sent them back to Earth. This gave scientists their first good look at this strange dwarf planet.

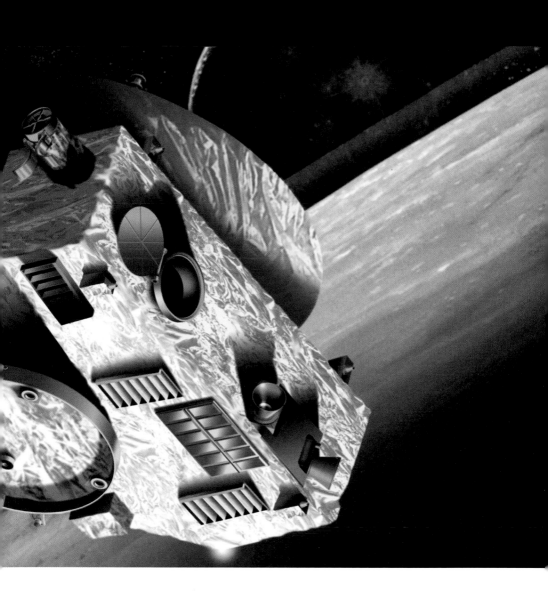

There's still a lot scientists don't know about Pluto. Maybe they will find even more moons orbiting Pluto, or rings like those that orbit Saturn. Some astronomers think there may be **cryovolcanoes** on Pluto and Charon that spew out ice.

Hubble Space Telescope—a satellite that observes things from space

space probe—an unmanned robotic spacecraft that is used to explore space

cryovolcanoes—cold volcanoes that erupt ice instead of molten rock

CHAPTER 5

Ceres—Dwarf Planet of the Asteroid Belt

Of the five known dwarf planets, Ceres is the only one located in the asteroid belt. Like Pluto, scientists are also learning more about Ceres as technology advances.

Ceres is the smallest known dwarf planet. It is only about 600 miles (1,000 km) across. That's about as wide as the state of Texas. Ceres is tiny compared to Earth, which is about 8,000 miles (12,900 km) across. Pictures of Ceres taken by a space probe show a gray surface with a lot of dust. The surface looks like our moon's. Small asteroids have crashed into Ceres, creating a lot of **craters**.

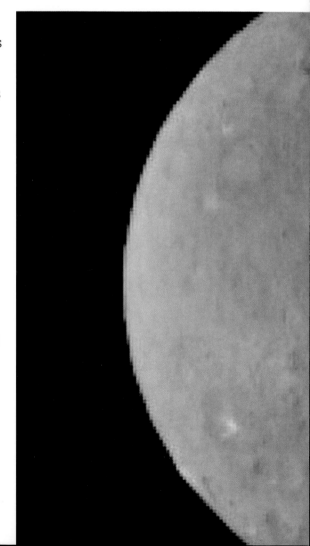

A NASA spacecraft captured this image of the dwarf planet Ceres on February 19, 2015.

Ceres is more than twice as far away from the sun as Earth. Sunlight can only warm its surface to about −36°F (−38°C). At that low temperature, the surface of Ceres is frozen solid. But some astronomers believe Ceres may have an ocean of liquid water under its frozen surface. Ceres also may have traces of a very thin **atmosphere** of water vapor. Frigid cryovolcanoes on the surface of Ceres could be erupting minerals and water **vapor**. At night on Ceres, the water in the atmosphere might be turning to snow and falling to the ground.

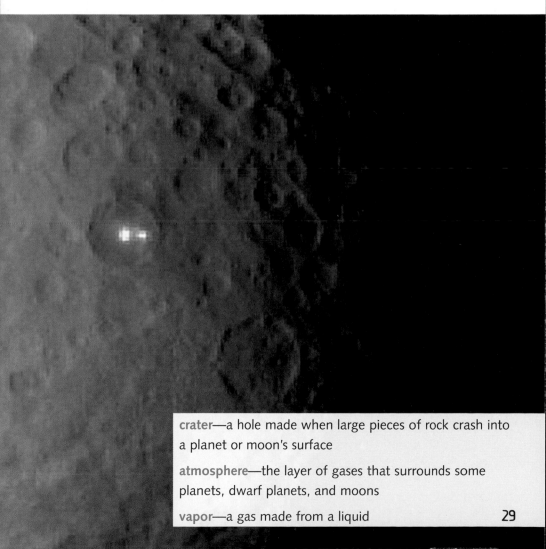

crater—a hole made when large pieces of rock crash into a planet or moon's surface

atmosphere—the layer of gases that surrounds some planets, dwarf planets, and moons

vapor—a gas made from a liquid

Scientists still have a lot of questions about Ceres. To help answer these questions, a space probe named *Dawn* is currently orbiting Ceres. NASA launched *Dawn* from Earth in 2007. It reached Ceres on March 5, 2015. Astronomers began getting close-up pictures of Ceres' surface. The pictures revealed a gray surface similar to Earth's moon and the planet Mercury. Unlike the moon and Mercury, however, nearly all the craters on Ceres are flattened. Scientists think this means the surface of Ceres is mostly soft ice rather than hard rock. The surface may have a thin layer of dust covering the ice.

Images of Ceres taken years earlier with the Hubble Space Telescope show strange bright spots against the gray surface. Cameras on *Dawn* captured these same bright spots. The photos show that the bright spots are near the centers of craters. Scientists studying the pictures noticed that the bright spots seem to extend into space, above the craters. They think the spots could be icy material escaping from cracks or cryovolcanoes on the dusty surface of Ceres. In other images from *Dawn*, scientists can see long cracks in Ceres' surface. Earthquakes form cracks like this on Earth. This could mean that Ceres has movements similar to those on Earth during earthquakes.

Dawn is currently orbiting Ceres. The spacecraft is sending photos back to scientists on Earth.

NASA SPACE PROBES

NASA stands for National Aeronautics and Space Administration. NASA's main job is to develop spacecraft to explore space. On September 27, 2007, NASA launched the space probe *Dawn*. *Dawn* is powered by solar panels that get energy from the sun. Its two cameras send pictures back to Earth using radio waves. It orbited the asteroid Vesta from 2011 to 2012. *Dawn* began its orbit of Ceres in March 2015.

CHAPTER 6

The Other Icy Dwarf Planets

Just as with Pluto and Ceres, scientists are learning more about the other three known dwarf planets every day.

Eris is nearly the same size as Pluto. Both are very far away from the sun, but Eris is much farther. Sometimes Eris moves closer to the sun. Eris does not orbit the sun in a circle, but in an **ellipse**. Right now Eris is about 100 times farther away from the sun than Earth is. That's about 10 billion miles (16 billion km). It takes Eris 557 Earth years to orbit the sun just one time. In that time Pluto has orbited the sun more than twice.

Eris orbits the sun in a long oval—not a circle like other objects orbit the sun.

ellipse—an orbit of a planet or space object in the shape of an oval

Eris

THE OUTER SOLAR SYSTEM

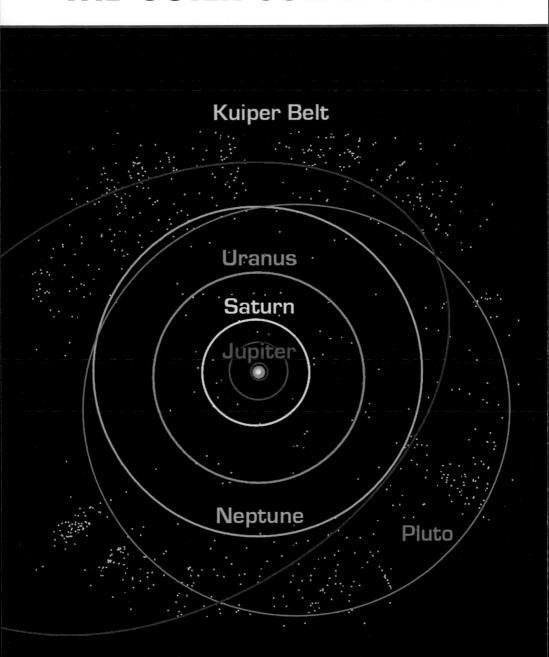

Kuiper Belt

Uranus

Saturn

Jupiter

Neptune

Pluto

When Eris is closest to the sun, it is about 40 times farther away than Earth is from the sun. At this distance Eris is a cold −400°F (−240°C). This temperature causes its atmosphere to completely freeze and fall onto its surface as snow. This layer of white snow gives Eris the brightest surface of all the dwarf planets. That extra brightness makes it easier for astronomers on Earth to spot Eris with their telescopes.

DWARF PLANET TECHNOLOGY

Discovering space objects is much easier today than it was for Clyde Tombaugh in 1930. Today cameras and telescopes are connected to computers. Images taken with cameras are sent directly to a computer. The computers automatically search thousands of images for faint objects moving slowly past the stars. This modern technology helped Mike Brown's team discover the dwarf planets Haumea, Makemake, and Eris. Brown's team wasn't the first to photograph these objects. Old pictures from the 1950s show all three. But without the help of new technology, nobody noticed them in the pictures back then.

Pictures of Eris show that it has a small moon. Astronomers study how this moon orbits around Eris to learn about the dwarf planet's gravity. By the strength of its gravity, they have learned that Eris is about half rock and half ice.

The distant sun and a moon can be seen in this artwork of the dwarf planet Eris.

Mike Brown and his team of astronomers discovered a big icy object on March 31, 2005. They could see the object orbit the sun in the frigid outer solar system beyond Neptune. They later named the object Makemake. Makemake is the second brightest object in the trans-neptunian region. Only Pluto is brighter.

NAMING MAKEMAKE

Before Makemake got an official name, astronomers nicknamed it the Easter Bunny. Mike Brown's team discovered Makemake just four days before Easter in 2005. Astronomers later gave the object the official name Makemake. Makemake was a god worshiped by the native people of Easter Island in the Pacific Ocean.

Fact

Makemake can be seen in photographs taken in 1955. Astronomers at the time didn't notice Makemake because it moves so slowly.

Makemake is about 52 times farther from the sun than Earth is. At such a large distance, Makemake takes about 310 Earth years to orbit the sun just once. It orbits the sun way out at the outer edge of the Kuiper belt. It is farther from the sun than Pluto. Eris is the only dwarf planet farther from the sun than Makemake. It is about twice as far away.

Makemake is the only dwarf planet in the trans-neptunian region that has no known moons. That makes it difficult for astronomers to figure out its size. Astronomers estimate that Makemake is about 900 miles (1,400 km) across, or about two-thirds the size of Pluto and Eris.

This artwork shows what the surface of Makemake may look like. The sun would look very small from the surface of Makemake.

Haumea is the third brightest trans-neptunian object, after Pluto and Makemake. After Mike Brown's team discovered Haumea, astronomers searched old pictures of the sky. They found that Haumea had been photographed several times before, starting in 1955.

Haumea is one of the strangest dwarf planets astronomers have ever seen. It is about two-thirds the size of Pluto. But Haumea spins much faster than any other planet or dwarf planet. It spins so fast that a day on Haumea lasts only 4 Earth hours. This fast spin makes Haumea look like a football. Astronomers know that if Haumea were not spinning so fast, it would be round. Because of the rule that dwarf planets are round, astronomers call Haumea a dwarf planet.

Fact

Discovered just three days after Christmas, on December 28, 2004, Mike Brown and his team nicknamed the new space object Santa. The official name later became Haumea, after a goddess of the native people of Hawaii.

From the surface of its moon Namaka, Haumea looks like an egg-shaped rock.

Two tiny moons, Hi'iaka and Namaka, orbit Haumea. By studying the motion of these moons, astronomers can tell what Haumea is made of. Haumea is made almost entirely of rock, with hardly any ice. Astronomers think nearly all the ice was blasted off Haumea in a big collision with another object. A collision may be what makes Haumea spin so fast.

New Discoveries

Today we know of five dwarf planets—Ceres, Pluto, Eris, Makemake, and Haumea. There are likely several more in our solar system waiting to be discovered.

Other objects in the trans-neptunian region might soon be considered dwarf planets. Scientists know that they orbit the sun near other objects. They must determine if the objects are round. Scientists have different ways of studying objects to find out if they are round.

FUTURE DWARF PLANETS

Four objects that soon might be considered dwarf planets are Sedna, Orcus, Quaoar, and Varuna. They all orbit the sun. They all have a lot of other objects near their orbit. Astronomers are studying these objects to determine if they are round. If they are round, they will be considered dwarf planets.

This illustration shows several space objects and their sizes in relation to Earth (on far right).

 Fact
Dwarf planets are tiny. All 10,000 that may exist could fit inside Earth, with room left over for about 5,000 more!

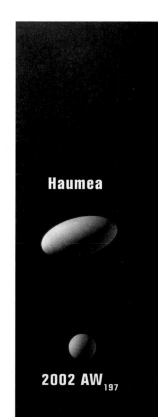
Haumea

2002 AW₁₉₇

Scientists can study the amount of sunlight that reflects off the surface of the object back toward Earth. If an object is covered in white frost but reflects a small amount of sunlight, then it may not be big and round. If an object is dark rock but reflects a large amount of sunlight, then it is probably big and round.

Scientists can also watch space objects pass in front of a distant star. Light from the star will be blocked as the object passes by. By timing how long the object blocks the starlight, astronomers can figure out the size and shape of the object.

Mike Brown's team has studied space objects this way. Brown believes that astronomers have already found 84 more round objects beyond Neptune, and possibly as many as 364. Brown thinks that as many as 10,000 more dwarf planets are still waiting to be discovered in our solar system!

Makemake   Sedna   Orcus   Quaoar   2002 TX$_{300}$

Varuna   Ixion   Vesta   Pallas   Hygiea

What we know about our universe is always changing. Astronomers are constantly discovering exciting new things. Sometimes new discoveries make us change our minds about what defines a planet. There may be only five dwarf planets today, but there are thousands of known objects in the trans-neptunian region. Billions more are waiting to be found. How many of them are round? Some day we could have 10,000 dwarf planets, or even more!

This chart shows the largest known trans-neptunian objects in comparison to Earth (at bottom).

BIGGER DWARF PLANETS

What happens if astronomers discover a round, trans-neptunian object larger than Earth? According to the three rules, it would just be a dwarf planet. But how can something bigger than Earth be just a dwarf planet when Earth itself is a planet? If this happens, astronomers may have to again reconsider what it means to be a planet in our solar system.

Makemake

Namaka

Hi'iaka

Haumea

Weywot

Quaoar

Vanth

Orcus

What would it be like to be on a dwarf planet instead of Earth?

Earth

current distance from sun (relative to Earth):	1
time to orbit once around sun:	1 year
length of a day:	24 hours
a 3rd grader's weight:	80 pounds (36 kg)
what object is made of:	rock and iron
main gases in atmosphere:	nitrogen, oxygen
number of moons:	1

Ceres

current distance from sun (relative to Earth):	2.7 times farther than Earth
time to orbit once around sun:	4.6 Earth years
length of a day:	9 Earth hours
a 3rd grader's weight:	2 pounds (0.9 kg)
what object is made of:	rock and ice
main gases in atmosphere:	water vapor?
number of moons:	0

Pluto

current distance from sun (relative to Earth):	32 times farther than Earth
time to orbit once around sun:	248 Earth years
length of a day:	154 Earth hours
a 3rd grader's weight:	5 pounds (2.3 kg)
what object is made of:	ice and rock
main gases in atmosphere:	nitrogen
number of moons:	5

Haumea

current distance from sun (relative to Earth):	50 times farther than Earth
time to orbit once around sun:	283 Earth years
length of a day:	4 Earth hours
a 3rd grader's weight:	3.5 pounds (1.6 kg)
what object is made of:	rock
main gases in atmosphere:	unknown
number of moons:	2

Makemake

current distance from sun (relative to Earth):	52 times farther than Earth
time to orbit once around sun:	310 Earth years
length of a day:	unknown
a 3rd grader's weight:	4 pounds (1.8 kg)?
what object is made of:	unknown
main gases in atmosphere:	unknown
number of moons:	0

Eris

current distance from sun (relative to Earth):	100 times farther than Earth
time to orbit once around sun:	557 Earth years
length of a day:	unknown
a 3rd grader's weight:	6.5 pounds (3 kg)
what object is made of:	ice and rock
main gases in atmosphere:	No atmosphere. Too cold!
number of moons:	1

Glossary

asteroid belt (AS-tuh-royd BELT)—the area in space between Mars and Jupiter where the most asteroids are found

atmosphere (AT-muh-sfeer)—the layer of gases that surrounds some planets, dwarf planets, and moons

crater (KRAY-tuhr)—a hole made when large pieces of rock crash into a planet or moon's surface

cryovolcanoes (kry-oh-vol-KAY-nohs)—cold volcanoes that erupt ice instead of molten rock

ellipse (ee-LIPS)—an orbit of a planet or space object in the shape of an oval

Hubble Space Telescope (hu-BELL SPAYSS TELL-uh-SCOPE)—a satellite that observes things from space

inner planets (IN-uhr PLAN-its)—the four planets closest to the sun—Mercury, Venus, Earth, and Mars

Kuiper belt (KOO-per BELT)—the area of the solar system between about 30 and 50 times farther from the sun than Earth

orbit (OR-bit)—the path an object follows as it goes around the sun or a planet

outer planets (OU-tur PLAN-its)—the four planets farthest from the sun—Jupiter, Saturn, Uranus, and Neptune

solar system (SOH-lur SISS-tuhm)—the sun and the objects that move around it

space probe (SPAYSS PROHB)—an unmanned robotic spacecraft that is used to explore space

trans-neptunian region (TRANSS-nep-TOON-ee-in REJ-uhn)—an area of space objects that orbit the sun beyond the planet Neptune

vapor (VAY-pur)— a gas made from a liquid

Critical Thinking Using the Common Core

1. Explain the difference between a planet and dwarf planet. Use evidence from the text to support your answer. (Key Idea and Details)

2. What if Pluto was still considered a planet? What other space objects could also be called planets? (Integration of Knowledge and Ideas)

3. Reread pages 8 through 11. Choose two parts of the solar system to compare and contrast. Explain how they are different and how they are similar. (Craft and Structure)

Read More

Glaser, Chaya. *Pluto: The Icy Dwarf Planet.* New York: Bearport Publishing Company, 2015.

Higgins, Nadia. *Dwarf Planets: Pluto and the Lesser Planets.* Inside Outer Space. Vero Beach, Fl.: Rourke Publishing, 2015.

Stewart, Kellie. *Journey to Pluto and Other Dwarf Planets.* Spotlight on Space Science. New York: PowerKids Press, 2015.

Internet Sites

FactHound offers a safe, fun way to find Internet sites related to this book. All of the sites on FactHound have been researched by our staff.

Here's all you do:

Visit *www.facthound.com*

Type in this code: 9781491441626

Check out projects, games and lots more at
www.capstonekids.com

Index